HOW DO WE LISTEN?

By JENNA LAFFIN

Illustrated by TINA KUGLER

CANTATA
LEARNING

MANKATO, MINNESOTA

WWW.CANTATALEARNING.COM

CANTATA
LEARNING
MANKATO, MINNESOTA

Published by Cantata Learning
1710 Roe Crest Drive
North Mankato, MN 56003
www.cantatalearning.com

Library of Congress Control Number: 2014956990
978-1-63290-258-0 (hardcover/CD)
978-1-63290-410-2 (paperback/CD)
978-1-63290-452-2 (paperback)

How Do We Listen? by Jenna Laffin
Illustrated by Tina Kugler

Book design by Tim Palin Creative
Editorial direction by Flat Sole Studio
Executive musical production and direction, Elizabeth Draper
Music arranged and produced by Musical Youth Productions

Printed in the United States of America.

VISIT
WWW.CANTATALEARNING.COM/ACCESS-OUR-MUSIC
TO SING ALONG TO THE SONG

You listen with your ears. Listening shows good **manners**. It means that you **respect** the person who is talking. Listening also helps you learn. If you don't listen while a teacher is giving instructions, then you may not know what to do.

Now turn the page, and sing along.

Oh, how do we listen?

Not with our toes or nose,

But we hear with our ears.

Oh, how do we listen?

With help from our eyes,

hands, and ears. It's clear!

In class, if I ignore my teacher
and talk to my friends,
I won't understand the **lesson**.

My learning will end.

But if I listen to
what my teacher tells me,
I might know the answer.
I bet 2 + 1 is 3!

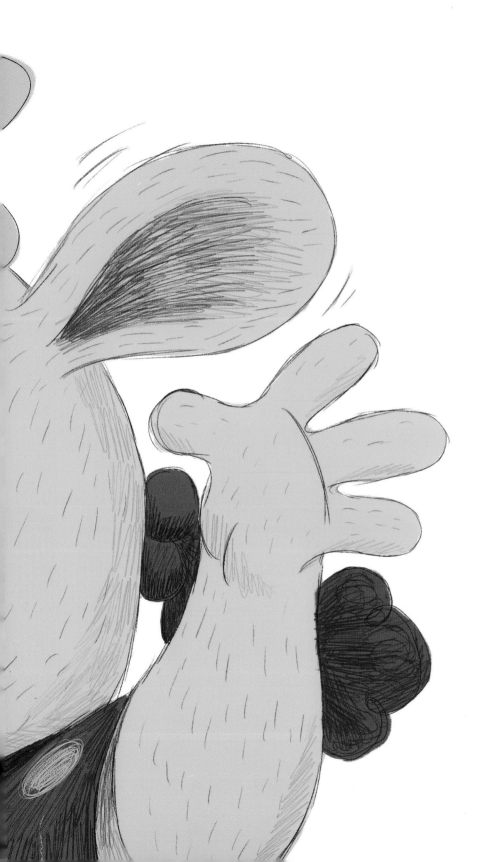

Oh, how do we listen?
Not with our toes or nose,
But we hear with our ears.

Oh, how do we listen?
With help from our eyes,
hands, and ears. It's clear!

When should we listen?

It's **polite** to listen all the time!

At the movies, with friends,

or walking around outside.

16

Why should we listen?

To show people we **respect** them.

Whether it's someone we don't know
or our grandparents.

Who should we listen to?

Just about everyone.

It shows we care,

and a good story is always fun.

Oh, how do we listen?

Not with our toes or nose,

But we hear with our ears.

Oh, how do we listen?

With help from our eyes,

hands, and ears. It's clear!

SONG LYRICS
How Do We Listen?

Oh, how do we listen?
Not with our toes or nose,
But we hear with our ears.

Oh, how do we listen?
With help from our eyes,
Hands, and ears. It's clear!

In class, if I ignore my teacher
and talk to my friends,
I won't understand the lesson.

My learning will end.

But if I listen to
what my teacher tells me,
I might know the answer.

I bet 2 + 1 is 3!

Oh, how do we listen?
Not with our toes or nose,
But we hear with our ears.

Oh, how do we listen?
With help from our eyes,
Hands, and ears. It's clear!

When should we listen?
It's polite to listen all the time!

At the movies, with friends,
or walking around outside.

Why should we listen?
To show people we respect them.

Whether it's someone we don't
    know
or our grandparents.

Who should we listen to?
Just about everyone.

It shows we care,
and a good story is always fun.

Oh, how do we listen?
Not with our toes or nose,
But we hear with our ears.

Oh, how do we listen?
With help from our eyes,
Hands, and ears. It's clear!

How Do We Listen?

Pop/Zydeco
Musical Youth Productions

Chorus

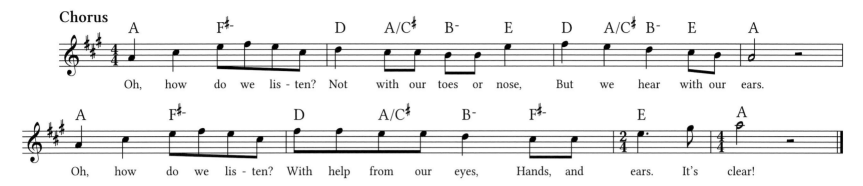

Oh, how do we lis-ten? Not with our toes or nose, But we hear with our ears.

Oh, how do we lis-ten? With help from our eyes, Hands, and ears. It's clear!

Verse 1

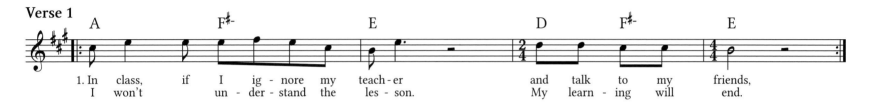

1. In class, if I ig-nore my teach-er and talk to my friends,
I won't un-der-stand the les-son. My learn-ing will end.

Verses 2-5

But if I lis-ten to what my teach-er tells me, I might know the an-swer. I bet 2 plus 1 is 3!

Chorus

Verse 3
When should we listen?
It's polite to listen all the time!
At the movies, with friends,
or walking around outside.

Verse 4
Why should we listen?
To show people we respect them.
Whether it's someone we don't know
or our grandparents.

Verse 5
Who should we listen to?
Just about everyone.
It shows we care,
and a good story is always fun.

Chorus

GLOSSARY

lesson—a learning activity

manners—the way someone behaves around other people

polite—showing good manners

respect—to treat someone as if he or she were important

GUIDED READING ACTIVITIES

1. What does the author teach us in this book?

2. We hear with our ears. But how do our eyes and hands help us listen?

3. Are there times you need to listen that are similar to examples in this story?

TO LEARN MORE

Burstein, John. *Have You Heard?: Active Listening*. New York: Crabtree Pub. Company, 2010.

Felix, Rebecca. *Good Manners with Your Friends*. Minneapolis: Magic Wagon, 2014.

Nelson, Maria. *I Can Listen*. New York: Gareth Stevens Publishing, 2014.

Nunn, Daniel. *I Can Listen*. Chicago: Capstone Heinemann Library, 2015.